Nelson Mandela

History Maker Bios

Judith Pinkerton Josephson

LERNER PUBLICATIONS COMPANY • MINNEAPOLIS

—For our brave daughter Erika

The pronunciation guide is based on *Nelson Mandela* by Reggie Finlayson in consultation with Martha Cosgrove, M.A. However, other guides may vary.

Lerner Publications Company
A division of Lerner Publishing Group, Inc.
241 First Avenue North
Minneapolis, MN 55401 USA

For reading levels and more information, look up this title at
www.lernerbooks.com.

Library of Congress Cataloging-in-Publication Data

Josephson, Judith Pinkerton.
  Nelson Mandela / by Judith P. Josephson.
      p.   cm. — (History maker biographies)
  Includes bibliographical references and index.
  ISBN 978-1-58013-703-4 (lib. bdg. : alk. paper)
      1. Mandela, Nelson, 1918– —Juvenile literature. 2. Presidents—South
  Africa—Biography—Juvenile literature. I. Title.
  DT1974.J675 2009
  968.06'5092—dc22 [B]   2008025151

Manufactured in the United States of America
4 – PC – 12/1/13

TABLE OF CONTENTS

INTRODUCTION

In 1918, the year Nelson Mandela was born, unjust laws limited the rights of black people in South Africa. When he grew up, Nelson became their voice. For his part in the freedom struggle, he spent twenty-seven years in a lonely island prison.

After his release, Nelson Mandela became South Africa's first black president. Son of a chief. Fighter for freedom. Father of a changed nation.

This is his story.

1 A VILLAGE CHILDHOOD

In a tiny South African village, a baby boy was born on July 18, 1918. Gadla Henry Mphakanyiswa (em-pah-gah-NEEZ-wah), the baby's father, was Ce tribe's chief. He and his wife named their son Rolihlahla (ho-lee-SHAH-shah) Mandela. In the Xhosa (KOH-sah) language, the name means "pulling the branch of a tree" or "troublemaker." He would become known as Nelson.

A tall, handsome man, the chief had dark brown skin and a patch of white hair above his forehead. Nelson rubbed white ash into his hair to look more like his father. The chief taught his son to fight for what was fair and right.

The chief was a trusted adviser to tribal rulers. Back then, white people controlled South Africa's government. Because of an argument with white officials, the chief lost his title, land, and wealth. Nelson's family moved to the village of Qunu (KOO-noo).

Nelson grew up in a Xhosa village like this one in South Africa.

PLAYING THINTI

Boys in Nelson's village often played the game of *thinti*. They pounded two posts into the ground yards apart. Two teams hurled sticks at each other's targets, hoping to knock them down and capture them. Boys who did well at this game became heroes.

His mother grew her own corn, called mealies. She boiled the corn or ground it into flour. Nelson hauled water and tended herds. Barefoot, he and friends ran in fields, slid down rocks, swam, and fished.

At seven, Nelson became the first in his family to attend school. Proudly, he wore his father's cutoff pants, the waist gathered with string. On the first day, the British teacher gave the children English names. That's when Rolihlahla became Nelson.

When Nelson was nine, his father died. This saddened him, but his mother's news seemed worse. She said Nelson must leave their village. Nelson did not understand.

Looking back at the village he had loved, Nelson wished he had kissed their three huts good-bye. On the journey, Nelson and his mother trudged up and down hills, past village after village. Finally, they reached the grand home of Chief Jongintaba (jun-geen-TAH-bah). His father's friend had offered to raise and educate the shy, serious boy. Nelson's mother returned to Qunu without him. Nelson settled into his new life. Justice, the chief's son, was four years older than Nelson. The two became as close as brothers.

Nelson lived in this hut under Jongintaba's care.

At school, ten-year-old Nelson studied English and Xhosa languages, African history, and geography. The chief taught Nelson about responsibility.

When Nelson turned sixteen, he and other boys took part in solemn ceremonies. The ceremonies marked their passage from boys to men. Storytellers told of brave warriors and powerful kings. But one speaker said that black South Africans were slaves in their own country. Nelson never forgot his words.

2 THE COUNTRY BOY WEARS BOOTS

Before Nelson left for Clarkebury Boarding Institute, a high school, the chief gave Nelson his first pair of boots. When Nelson clomped awkwardly into a classroom, girls giggled. One said loudly, "The country boy is not used to wearing shoes."

The chief introduced Nelson to the stern white director of the school, the Reverend Cecil Harris. He agreed to let the young man work in his private garden. Soon, Nelson shared the director's love for gardening.

At nineteen, Nelson went on to Healdtown, a religious college. Classes, studying, meals, and exercise filled his days. Tall and strong, Nelson loved running and spending time alone. New experiences

and new ways of thinking surprised Nelson. At school, he made friends with a boy from another tribe. He saw a black housemaster stand up to the school's white director.

By the end of college, Nelson already showed signs of leadership.

Students study at the University College at Fort Hare in the early 1940s.

At twenty-one, Nelson entered University College at Fort Hare. The chief bought Nelson his first suit. He got used to flush toilets, hot showers, soap, and pajamas. Instead of using toothpicks and ash to clean his teeth, he used a toothbrush and toothpaste.

Nelson missed the simple country ways. Some nights, he and his friends roasted mealies in a cornfield and told tall tales. At the university, Nelson was a good boxer and long-distance runner. Nelson made a good friend in Oliver Tambo, a serious young man and great debater.

DANCING LESSONS

At University College, Nelson and his friends learned ballroom dancing. The young men took turns leading and following. But they longed to practice with female partners. So one night, they put on their good suits and sneaked out to a popular black dance hall. Students weren't allowed there, but Nelson and his friends talked their way in. Nelson finally got the chance to whirl a pretty woman around the dance floor.

University College was South Africa's only black university. But in town, Nelson and his friends couldn't eat in white restaurants. White people looked down on black people, regardless of their education or abilities.

In 1941, twenty-three-year-old Nelson went home for a visit. The chief told Nelson and Justice that he feared he would die soon. So he had chosen brides for each of them. The weddings would take place immediately.

Nelson hated to disobey, but he and Justice wanted to choose their own wives. The young men decided to run away to Johannesburg. For travel money, they secretly sold two of the chief's prize cattle.

Neither had the proper travel papers required for black people to board a train. So they paid an elderly white woman to let them ride along to Johannesburg in the backseat of her car. The closer they got, the more cars filled the road. Electric lights glittered. Tall buildings loomed. The woman let the exhausted young men sleep in the servants' quarters at her daughter's Johannesburg mansion. Excitement about the days to come raced through Nelson.

3 THE STRUGGLE BEGINS

Johannesburg overflowed with people, but race divided the city. Hospitals, buses, schools, and housing for black people were separate from those used by white people. Nelson thought this was wrong.

Many black people worked as house servants or miners. Underground mining work was dangerous and dirty. By mentioning the chief's name, Nelson and Justice got easier, aboveground jobs. When the chief heard about this, he told the mine boss to fire them and send them home. They lost their jobs but stayed on in the city.

Through Walter Sisulu, a black businessman, Nelson found work as a law clerk. He moved into a dingy room in a crowded black slum and took university classes by mail. Sisulu also gave Nelson one of his old suits. Nelson wore it every day. He patched the threadbare suit until there were more patches than suit.

PASS LAWS

Until 1986, Black South Africans sixteen years or older had to carry a native passbook at all times. It listed their address, their chief's name, and an employer's signature.

Chief Jongintaba (LEFT) and Walter Sisulu (RIGHT) were two important role models in Nelson's life.

In late 1941, the chief visited Nelson. They made their peace. When the chief died six months later, Nelson and Justice traveled home. Justice would take his father's place as chief. Nelson chose not to stay on and become his adviser.

Back in the city, Nelson moved closer to Sisulu's home. Other young, black South Africans gathered there. Many belonged to the African National Congress (ANC), a group fighting racism. One was Oliver Tambo, Nelson's college friend.

Determined to change things for his people, Nelson enrolled in law school in Johannesburg. One professor said he didn't believe blacks or women were smart enough to study law. Still, Nelson found others who believed in freedom and equal rights for all people. He joined ten thousand people in a bus boycott against rising bus fees.

In 1944, twenty-six-year-old Nelson married nursing student Evelyn Mase in a simple ceremony. Their small house had a tin roof and a cement floor and no electricity or plumbing. But the young couple was in love and alone together. A year later, their son Thembi (TEM-bee) was born. Nelson loved playing hide-and-seek with Thembi and reading him stories.

Nelson, Evelyn, and Thembi lived in a black township like this one (separate area for blacks) outside Johannesburg.

Nelson (RIGHT) listens at an ANC Youth League meeting.

Soon Nelson Mandela, Walter Sisulu, and Oliver Tambo formed the Youth League as part of the ANC. As a speaker, Nelson's words offered ordinary people hope for the future. Nelson later said there was no one moment when he decided to dedicate his life to the struggle for freedom. But each step brought him closer.

4 FIGHTING FOR FREEDOM

In time, the Mandelas had another son, Makgatho (ma-gha-THOO), and daughter, Makaziwe (mah-kah-ZEE-weh).

Over the next six years, Nelson's job, studies, and activities demanded his time. Boxing took his mind off his people's struggle for freedom. Yet that same struggle pulled him away from his family. One day, five-year-old Thembi asked where his daddy lived. Nelson's work had caused him to come home after the child was asleep and leave before he awoke.

After law school, Nelson began work as a full-time attorney. This gave him self-confidence and the respect of others.

In the 1948 elections, the policy of apartheid, or "apartness," became law. This law separated nonwhites from whites and gave fewer rights to black South Africans. Already, black South Africans could not vote or own land. One unjust law said that black South Africans could not walk on sidewalks in white areas. In 1952, Nelson helped organize a protest. Black South Africans purposely used "Whites Only" toilets or entered white sections of post offices or railway cars.

Protesters ride a "EUROPEANS ONLY" train car in 1952.

Nelson stands in his Johannesburg law office in the early 1950s.

Many people were arrested. Nelson and other leaders spent two days in a filthy prison.

Also in 1952, Nelson Mandela and Oliver Tambo formed Johannesburg's first black law firm. Tambo was quiet and calm. Mandela was dramatic and powerful. People came to court just to hear him speak about civil rights. He won many cases.

In 1953, thirty-five-year-old Nelson took part in the ongoing protests. So the government banned him from attending meetings or political gatherings.

Nelson and Oliver Tambo helped write a Freedom Charter in 1955. It demanded equality for all. The Freedom Charter became the blueprint for South Africa's freedom struggle.

THE FREEDOM CHARTER

Protesters carved the Freedom Charter into the wall of a court waiting room.

1. The people shall govern!
2. All national groups shall have equal rights!
3. The people shall share in the country's wealth!
4. The land shall be shared among those who work it!
5. All shall be equal before the law!
6. All shall enjoy equal human rights!
7. There shall be work and security!
8. The doors of learning and culture shall be opened!
9. There shall be houses, security, and comfort!
10. There shall be peace and friendship!

Evelyn had become deeply religious. She began to resent her husband's political activities. In late 1956, Nelson, thirty-eight, went to the countryside alone. He visited family and friends and thought about his life.

Soon after Nelson returned, he and several ANC leaders were arrested. The charge was treason, or plotting to overthrow the government. They were released when bail money was paid. They would return later to stand trial. Nelson returned home to an empty house. Evelyn had left him, taking their children with her. Their marriage was over.

Nelson appears outside the building where he was tried for treason from 1956 to 1960.

5 TEN THOUSAND DAYS IN PRISON

Soon, Nelson fell in love with a black social worker called Winnie. She was beautiful, well educated, and rebellious. They married on June 14, 1958. Their family grew when two daughters, Zenani (zen-AHN-nee) and Zindziswa (zin-ZEE-swa) were born.

Nelson continued fighting for equal rights. Over the next few years, he was arrested and jailed several times. Charges in the treason trial were dropped. But government spies followed him almost everywhere. In 1961, he began living a secret life. Wearing disguises to fool the spies, he moved from one house to another. He continued his ANC work. Then he sneaked out of the country.

In 1962, Nelson (LEFT) went to Algeria to meet with leaders of the Algerian army and the ANC.

When he returned on August 4, 1962, he was arrested again. This time, Nelson and other ANC members, including Walter Sisulu, were charged with sabotage, or working to violently overthrow the government. Nelson had also left the country illegally. Winnie visited him in jail. They hugged and kissed, fighting back tears. Neither of them imagined just how long they would be apart.

The trial began in 1963. Several months later, the defendants were found guilty. Before sentencing, Nelson told the court he was willing to die for his ideal of a democratic and free society.

Nelson found power in wearing traditional Xhosa clothing during his trial in 1962.

This was Nelson's cell at Robben Island prison.

On June 12, 1964, the judge sentenced eight of the accused, including Nelson, to life in prison. Forty-six-year-old Nelson Mandela became Prisoner 466/64 on bleak Robben Island, South Africa's toughest prison. The walls of the tiny cells were cold and damp. Prisoners slept on straw mats covered by thin blankets. Most meals were mealie pap porridge, a corn cereal. Rarely did prisoners have meat or vegetables.

SHORT PANTS FOR PRISONERS

Even though prisoners on Robben Island were grown men, officials made them wear short pants. Nelson Mandela refused. Only children wore short pants at that time. Finally, officials gave him long pants. But they sent him to solitary confinement. Locked up in a cell alone, he had nothing to read or do. He later convinced officials to let all prisoners wear long pants.

On their few visiting days, prisoners could not touch loved ones or talk in their native tribal language. They had to speak either English or Afrikaans, then the official language of South Africa. Guards always listened in. Officials read all letters from loved ones first, crossing out parts they didn't like. Some letters never even reached the prisoners or their families.

Every day, prisoners worked at a limestone rock quarry. With picks, they chipped the limestone from hard rock.

No sunglasses protected their eyes. Limestone dust covered their bodies. To lighten the work, prisoners sang about the freedom struggle. To stay strong, Nelson ran in place, did exercises, and walked around the courtyard.

In spring 1968, Nelson's mother visited. She looked thin and tired. Several weeks later, he learned she had died from a heart attack. "It added to my grief that I was not able to bury my mother, which was my responsibility as her only son," he said.

Prisoners worked splitting rocks in the Robben Island prison yard.

Winnie had tried to carry on Nelson's work. She gave fiery speeches and joined protests against apartheid. In 1969, she was arrested and questioned about her activities. Police beat her to force her to answer. She spent months in jail. Nelson longed to be with her and their children.

Later that year, Nelson learned that his twenty-five-year-old son, Thembi, had died in a car accident. Nelson lay in his cell, wrapped in a blanket. His friends tried to help, but sadness overcame Nelson.

Somehow, he went on. He planted a courtyard garden, a source of joy. Both prisoners and guards enjoyed the fresh fruits and vegetables he grew.

Winnie (SECOND FROM LEFT) was arrested many times during the years Nelson was in prison.

Nelson (LEFT) worked for the rights of other prisoners while he was in jail.

Nelson often spoke for the other prisoners, asking officials for fair treatment. Prisoners received desks and books so they could study. Because of him, Robben Island became a place of learning. Men even staged plays.

Prisoners weren't allowed to read newspapers, news magazines, or political books. Instead, Nelson read mysteries, law books, and novels about great leaders.

Other prisoners admired Nelson's strength, courage, and endurance. Nelson told them never to give up.

6 AT LAST, FREEDOM!

On Robben Island, days melted into weeks, months, and years. Prison had made fifty-seven-year-old Nelson appreciate every blade of grass and every flower that bloomed. Events and people from his life before prison filled his thoughts.

In 1975, Nelson's friends suggested he write about his life. Night after night, Nelson wrote. One friend copied the memoir in tiny writing.

Another took that copy with him when he left prison. Nelson and two others buried the five-hundred-page original in three places in the garden. Prison guards found part of it. The three friends lost study privileges for the next four years.

In 1978, Nelson and Winnie's daughter Zeni and her husband visited with Nelson's granddaughter Zaziwe (zah-ZEE-weh), meaning "hope." When this baby grew up, Nelson, sixty, hoped life would be better for black South Africans.

Nelson's daughter Zindziswa (RIGHT, WITH SIGN) fought for her father's release from prison.

Riots broke out in Soweto, South Africa, in 1977. Rioters were protesting government policies.

For some time, prisoners had heard rumors of a great uprising in the country. Stone-throwing black youths battled riot police. Some young freedom fighters were sent to Robben Island. Nelson urged these "young lions" to study and learn.

Nelson, sixty-four, now suffered from lung problems and high blood pressure. Some guards were cruel. Others were kind. Nelson worked with them all to improve prison conditions.

In Britain, Oliver Tambo had started a Free Mandela campaign that had spread to South Africa. Pressure grew worldwide for South Africa to end its racist policy of apartheid.

A concert for Nelson's seventieth birthday was staged to demand his release and the end of apartheid in South Africa.

In March 1982, Nelson Mandela, Walter Sisulu, and others were moved to a prison in Cape Town. Rooms had real beds. Prisoners could read magazines and newspapers. Meals included meat and fresh vegetables. Nelson planted a garden with nine hundred plants. Best of all, two years later, visiting rules relaxed. For the first time in twenty-one years, he hugged and kissed his wife, Winnie. He never wanted to let her go. In 1988, Mandela was moved

to a small cottage at another prison. Barbed wire topped the fence. A guard stood at the door. But hope blossomed in Nelson's heart.

Winnie (LEFT) and a friend arrive at a Cape Town prison to visit Nelson.

He dared to hope that one day he and his people would be free. Nelson's access to the outside world increased. Other countries urged South Africa to release its political prisoners. In October 1989, Sisulu and the others were freed. Only Nelson remained.

On Sunday, February 11, 1990, a huge crowd gathered. Seventy-one-year-old Nelson Mandela smiled broadly—a dignified man, his mind keen and clear. Cameras clicked. Then, fist in the air, he walked from prison. Free at last!

Nelson and his wife, Winnie, celebrate his freedom.

Nelson (CENTER), Winnie (LEFT), and Walter Sisulu (RIGHT) sing "God Bless Africa" at a 1993 ANC event celebrating Nelson's release.

"I felt that my life was beginning anew. My ten thousand days of imprisonment were over," he said.

Nelson and Winnie returned to Johannesburg to the same small house he had left twenty-seven years before. He was free. But black South Africans still could not vote. The country was not yet a free democracy. He became active again in the ANC.

Prison had robbed Nelson of countless tender moments as a son, father, and husband. Winnie had suffered greatly too. He still loved her. But in 1992, Nelson announced they would divorce.

In 1993, Nelson built himself a country house in Qunu, his beloved childhood village. That same year, he shared the Nobel Peace Prize with South Africa's president, F. W. de Klerk. Despite their differences, they had worked out a historic agreement to end apartheid. The country's new constitution included all citizens.

Nelson Mandela (LEFT) and F. W. de Klerk receive the 1993 Nobel Peace Prize in Oslo, Norway.

The memoir Nelson had started in prison, *Long Walk to Freedom*, was published in 1994. That spring, his close friend Oliver Tambo died. Nelson felt part of himself had also died.

When South Africa held its first free, democratic election, people of all races voted. On May 10, 1994, at age seventy-five, Nelson Mandela became the country's president.

Nelson casts his vote in South Africa's first all-race election in 1994.

Nelson takes the oath of office to become South Africa's first black president.

Nelson's four living children had grown up without their father. "To be the father of a nation is a great honor, but to be the father of a family is a greater joy," Nelson later wrote. "But it was a joy I had far too little of. . . . I have walked that long road to freedom, but with freedom comes responsibility." He remained president until 1999.

This fearless, big-hearted man, whose childhood name meant "troublemaker," had changed history and helped bring equality to South Africa. Son of a chief, Nelson Mandela fought for freedom and became the father of a changed nation.

TIMELINE

In the year . . .

1925   Nelson entered school in Qunu.

1927   his father died, and Chief Jongintaba became his guardian.

1934   Nelson attended Clarkebury Boarding Institute.

1939   he attended University College at Fort Hare.   Age 21

1941   he ran away to Johannesburg.

1943   he graduated from college, went to law school, and joined the ANC.

1944   he married Evelyn Mase.   Age 26

1948   apartheid became law.

1953   he was banned from political meetings.   Age 35

1955   he and Walter Sisulu wrote the Freedom Charter.

1958   Nelson and Evelyn divorced. He married Nomzamo Winnie Madikizela.

1964   he was sentenced to life in prison.   Age 46

1975   he wrote his autobiography.

1982   he was moved to Pollsmoor and Victor Verster prisons.

1990   he left prison.   Age 71

1992   he and Winnie separated. They later divorce.

1993   he shared the Nobel Peace Prize with South Africa's president, F. W. de Klerk.

1994   Nelson became president of South Africa.

1998   he married Graça Machel.   Age 90

2008   thousands celebrated his ninetieth birthday on July 18. He spoke out about injustice, the AIDS epidemic, and other important issues.

LIFE AFTER PRISON

At the Nelson Mandela Foundation Centre, visitors learn about the life of this brave man. They view photos and exhibits and read his speeches and prison letters. To his children, he wrote, "One day . . . I will come back and live happily together with you in one house, sit at table together, help you with the many problems you will experience as you grow." Letters that officials censored or kept were held in Nelson's prison file until his release.

In 1998, on his eightieth birthday, Nelson married for the third time. He married Graça Machel (*right, with Nelson in 1998*). Since then, his dear friend Walter Sisulu and Nelson's son Makgatho have died. Retired now, Nelson still rises early and exercises. In 2004, he carried the torch for the Olympic Games. For the first time, since the modern Olympics began, the torch had reached South African soil. These days, he enjoys being

at home with his family. Among his favorite pastimes are listening to music and watching the sunset—simple pleasures denied to him during his long years in prison.

FURTHER READING

Cooper, Floyd. *Mandela: From the Life of the South African Statesman.* **New York: Puffin Books, 1996.** Read more about Nelson Mandela in this beautifully illustrated book.

Dennenberg, Barry. *Nelson Mandela: No Easy Walk to Freedom.* **New York: Scholastic, 2005.** Dig deeper into the history of South Africa and the life of Nelson Mandela.

Mantell, Paul. *Arthur Ashe: Young Tennis Champion.* **New York: Aladdin, 2006.** Read about this African American tennis star, who was a Mandela admirer.

WEBSITES

Apartheid Museum
http://www.apartheidmuseum.org Learn more about apartheid at this site.

The Long Walk of Nelson Mandela
http://www.pbs.org/wgbh/pages/frontline/shows/mandela Read interviews and Mandela quotes.

Nelson Mandela Foundation
http://www.nelsonmandela.org Visit this website for Nelson Mandela information.

Nelson Rolihlahla (Madiba) Mandela
http://www.sahistory.org.za/pages/people/bios/mandela-n .htm Find out more about Nelson Mandela.

Nobel Prize
http://nobelprize.org/nobel_prizes/peace/laureates/1993/ mandela-bio.html Read about Nelson Mandela as a winner of the Nobel Peace Prize.

Radio Series
http://www.mandelahistory.org/ Listen to a five-part radio series about Nelson Mandela's life.

The TIME 100
http://www.time.com/time/time100/leaders/profile/ mandela.html Read the article naming him as one of that year's one hundred best leaders in the world.

SELECT BIBLIOGRAPHY

African National Congress. "Profile of Nelson Rolihlahla Mandela" *ANC.* N.d. http://www.anc.org.za/people/ mandela.html (July 2, 2008).

Asmal, Kader, David Chidester, and Wilmot James, eds. *Nelson Mandela: In His Own Words.* New York: Little Brown and Company, 2003.

Maharaj, Mac, and Ahmed Kathrada, eds. *Mandela: The Authorized Portrait.* Kansas City, MO: Andrews McMeel Publishing, 2006.

Mandela, Nelson. *A Long Walk to Freedom.* New York: Little, Brown and Company, 1995.

Nelson Mandela Foundation. *A Prisoner in the Garden.* New York: Viking Studio, 2006.

Tutu, Desmond. *No Future without Forgiveness.* New York: Random House, 1999.

INDEX

Acknowledgments

For photographs and artwork: © Dave Hogan/Getty Images, p. 4; © UWC-Robben Island Museum Mayibuye Archives, pp. 7, 9, 12, 13, 20, 27, 28, 31, 33; © The McGregor Museum/The Duggan-Cronin Collection, p. 18 (left); © Jurgen Schadeberg/Premium Archive/Getty Images, pp. 18 (right), 23, 25; © Pat English/Time & Life Pictures/Getty Images, p. 19; © Bettmann/CORBIS, p. 22; © travelstock44/Alamy, p. 29; AP Photo, pp. 32, 36; © Gideon Mendel/AFP/Getty Images, p. 35; AP Photo/Str/Gillian Allen, p. 37; AP Photo/Adil Bradlow, p. 38; © Allan Tannenbaum/ZUMA Press, p. 39; AP Photo/Udo Weitz, p. 40; AP Photo/NTB, p. 41; AP Photo/John Parkin, p. 42; AP Photo/David Brauchli, p. 43; AP Photo/Benny Gool, p. 45.

Front Cover: AP Photo/CP, Fred Chartrand.

Back Cover: © Laura Westlund/Independent Picture Service.

For quoted material: pp. 11, 31, 40, 43, Nelson Mandela, *A Long Walk to Freedom* (New York: Little Brown and Company, 1995); p. 45, Ahmed Kathrada and Mac Maharaj, ed. consultants, *Mandela: The Authorized Portrait* (Kansas City, MO: Andrews McMeel Publishing, 2006).